The
GARDENS *of* TUSCANY

The GARDENS *of* TUSCANY

Text by ETHNE CLARKE

Photographs by RAFFAELLO BENCINI

WEIDENFELD AND NICOLSON
LONDON

For Rosemary, who initiated the education of this gardener, and to whom I shall always be grateful.

     Ethne Clarke
     Norfolk, January 1990

First published in 1990 by
George Weidenfeld & Nicolson Ltd
91 Clapham High Street, London SW4 7TA

British Library Cataloguing in Publication data
Clarke, Ethne
  The gardens of Tuscany.
  1. Italy. Gardens, to 1960
  I Title.   II. Bencini, Raffaello
712.60945

  ISBN 0-297-83044-9

p. 1: I Collazzi, near Florence (see also p. 74)

p. 2: Castello di Uzzano (see also pp. 22–5)

❧ CONTENTS ❧

ACKNOWLEDGMENTS

We would like to thank the following people for admitting us to their gardens and for their generous help with the production of this book:

Principe and Principessa Torrigiani-Colonna (Villa Torrigiani); Principessa Giorgiana Corsini; Marchese Torrigiani di Santa Cristina and Marchese Torrigiani Malaspina (Giardino Torrigiani); Contessa Thea Brughiere; Conte Giovanni Guicciardini; Conti Castelbarco Albani Masetti and Marion de Jacobert; Conti Ginori Lisci; Barone Giovanni Ricasoli; Sir Harold Acton; Rev Donald Freeze, S.J. Provost, Georgetown University; Notaro Giovanni Guiso; Miss Heidi Boardman; Signora Fiorella Superbi and the Harvard Centre for Renaissance Studies; Signora Anna Marchi Mazzini; Signora Barbara Benelli; Signora Luiga Benelli Bellandi; Signor and Signora Scarselli; Signor Giulio Petroni and Signora Loredana Lenzi; Signora Marie Louise Schoharl; the family Nieuwenkamp-Bramante; Mr Teddy Millington-Drake; Fratelli Masini s.n.c., Societa Metallurgica Italiana; The Garden Club of Florence. Special thanks are due to Signor Giorgio Calligaris and to all of Brenda and Raffaello's many friends who provided us with countless contacts, valuable advice and warm and welcome hospitality.

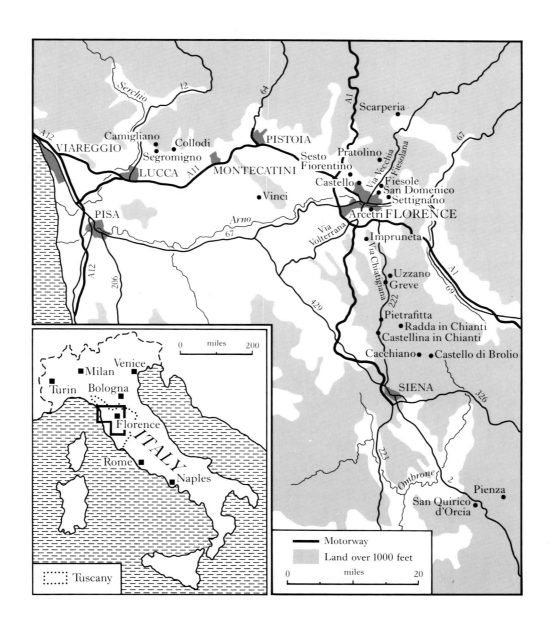

Serchio

12

64

A12

Camigliano
Collodi
VIAREGGIO
Segromigno
LUCCA
A11

PISTOIA

A1

Scarperia

Sesto
Fiorentino
Pratolino

MONTECATINI

Castello
Via Vecchia
Fiesolana
Fiesole
San Domenico
Settignano

Vinci

Arcetri FLORENCE

PISA

Arno

67

Via
Volterrana

Via Chiantigiana

Impruneta

67

A1

69

Uzzano
Greve

222

429

Pietrafitta
Radda in Chianti
Castellina in Chianti

Cacchiano
Castello di Brolio

SIENA

326

223

Ombrone

2

Pienza

San Quirico
d'Orcia

0   miles   200

Venice
Milan
Turin
Bologna
Florence

ITALY

Rome

Naples

Tuscany

— Motorway

Land over 1000 feet

0   miles   20

❧ FOREWORD ❧

VILLA PALMIERI
FIESOLE

The Victorian gardens of the
Villa Palmieri, seen from the
terrace, include a swimming
pool overlooked by a *loggetta*
and a tennis court which are
reached via an arbour covered
in *Rosa banksiae* 'Lutea'.
Within the grounds is another
smaller villa, the gardens of
which were designed by the
modern landscape designer
Pietro Porcinai, which brings
this particular Tuscan garden
full circle, encompassing as it
does the main periods of
architectural and landscape
design from the Renaissance to
the contemporary in four
distinct areas. See also pp.
107–10.

A TRUE GARDEN-LOVER with far more knowledge of plants and flowers than most of us possess, Ethne Clarke is admirably equipped to evoke the peculiar Tuscan magic which has played so important a part in my existence since early childhood.

Evidently ladies are more acutely sensitive than gentlemen in their appreciation of Italian gardens. Janet Ross, Edith Wharton, Vernon Lee (Violet Paget) and Georgina Masson were Ethne Clarke's pioneering predecessors when travel was more arduous and the roads to Tuscan villas were more rugged. Edith Wharton dedicated her enthusiastic *Italian Villas and their Gardens* (1904) to Vernon Lee 'who, better than any one else, has understood and interpreted the garden-magic of Italy'. With due apologies to her successor Ethne Clarke and allowing for the lapse of time, this remains true.

Italian gardens, which depend mainly on their architectural design, require ample leisure to cultivate, if not to appreciate, their characteristic virtues, and most foreign visitors seem to be in a frantic hurry. They arrive with their cameras, which are too often their mechanical substitutes for vision: clickety-click and off they go, having 'done' yet another beauty-spot.

Like Edith Wharton and Vernon Lee at the beginning of this century, Ethne Clarke has taken pains to visit the most beautiful gardens of Tuscany, both private and public. These, as Vernon Lee observed, do not depend on horticulture, though she strained the point when she added: 'Gardens have nothing to do with Nature, or not much.' Ethne Clarke amends this quaint paradox in her studious survey of the gardens of Tuscany. She reminds us that English colonists are still restoring ancient farms, as at Cacchiano where 'entire terraces are given over to solid plantings of iris and lavender' and there is 'a mixed border terrace of silver-leafed shrubs such as phlomis, senecio, cistus and sage, interspersed with pink roses'.

The early Medici, who were deeply attached to their native soil, set admirable examples at their country residences of Cafaggiolo, Careggi, Castello, Petraia, Poggio a Caiano, and later at Pratolino, most of which have been vividly recorded by Giuseppe Zocchi, the eighteenth-century engraver, but few of these retain their pristine charm. The majority illuminate the history of Florence's remote past, the prolonged domination of the Medici and the exceptional independence of Lucca, whose landscape has changed so little since Montaigne visited it in the sixteenth century, though few of its former gardens survive except those of Villa Mansi and Villa Torrigiani. The flower market is still active at Pistoia, and the magnificent Villa Garzoni at Collodi near Pescia, with its exuberant sequence of pools and terraces, 'built against a hillside, with wonderful waterworks which give you shower-baths when you expect them least', continues to astound the modern spectator.

Of the villas nearer Florence I should award the palm to the exquisite Gamberaia near Settignano, beyond Bernard Berenson's renovated Villa I Tatti, which he bequeathed to Harvard for students of art history. Since it belonged to the Gambarelli family which produced the famous Rossellino sculptor-architects Antonio and Bernardo in the fifteenth century, the Villa Gamberaia passed into the hands of the Capponi family in the eighteenth century, when Giuseppe Zocchi engraved it, but alas! he failed to illustrate the garden, which was restored, if not transformed, by Princess Ghika, sister of Queen Natalia of Serbia, who filled the parterre pools with shimmering sheets of water enlivened by long-tailed Chinese goldfish. The house and garden were disastrously ruined during the last world war but the present owner Dr Marchi has restored them to perfection. We can only endorse Georgina Masson's opinion that 'today the garden is at once the loveliest and the most typically Tuscan that the writer has seen'.

The spirit of Boccaccio still haunts the Villa Palmieri, a refuge from the devouring plague in the fourteenth century and now a refuge from clamorous motor-traffic. The distinguished scholar and crony of the elder Cosimo de' Medici, Matteo Palmieri, for whom Botticelli painted the *Assumption of the Virgin*, now in London's National Gallery, to illustrate Palmieri's poem 'The City of Life', bought the property in 1454, since when it remained an intellectual centre, belonging in the eighteenth century to the sophisticated Earl of Cowper, after whom it passed into the hands of the Earl of Crawford and Balcarres. By the time Queen Victoria chose to stay in Florence there was a considerable British colony, but this has dwindled since two world wars. Two English architects, Cecil Pinsent and Geoffrey Scott, collaborated in the revival of Tuscan gardens at I Tatti and Le Balze. The Villa Medici at Fiesole, built *c.* 1458–1461 on the hillside with a fabulous view over Florence, seems to have changed little since its creation, and we may well imagine Lorenzo the Magnificent discoursing with his friends of the Platonic Academy on the verdant terrace. Approached by a conventional alley of cypresses, the garden has never been drastically altered and the spectacular view is perennial.

'Even in their decay and faded grandeur,' as Ethne Clarke so touchingly observes in this illustrative volume, these Tuscan villas and gardens have 'caused many cold northern hearts to flutter'. While reading her sympathetic survey I felt as enthusiastic as if I were revisiting these tranquil habitations on a brilliant sunny day, or by the light of a harvest moon. The most obstinate stay-at-home will surely be tempted to follow in Ethne Clarke's footsteps.

Summer and winter elicit harmonies of colour and composition undreamt of, as surprising as the eighteenth-century shower baths at Collodi.

Harold Acton

❦ INTRODUCTION ❦

I TATTI
SETTIGNANO

The gardens at I Tatti, which are perfectly attuned to their setting and devoid of unnecessary detail, are evidence of the breadth of vision of their architect, Cecil Pinsent. To balance the patterning of the box hedges and the traditional stone mosaic work of the paving, he filled the parterres with plain grass rather than brightly coloured flowers. On the lowest terrace the uniformity is relieved by twin sheets of water in rectangular pools, reflecting the azure sky. See also pp. 123–8.

M Y GREAT-GRANDMOTHER, Emma Reuss, was a world-traveller. At a time when most women of her generation were just beginning to loosen their stays, she had already traversed the globe. She saw most of Europe, then went to Japan, and next tried living in Brazil (where she made a bad marriage to a German count who lost all her money for her on a speculative venture, growing oranges outside Rio de Janeiro). Emma finished her days in Milwaukee, Wisconsin, turning the pages of the albums full of souvenir postcards she had collected. Looking through dance cards from festivities aboard the steamships she had travelled on, she would snap open, with a puff of dust, the sequinned fans she had flirted over. Then her gaze would turn wistfully to the herbarium she had made from the leaves, blossoms, mosses and ferns that decorated the landscapes she once passed through. The most beautiful pages, for I now own this album, are those titled 'Florence', 'Siena', 'Lucca', 'Fiesole'. There lie brittle posies of yellowed jasmine blossoms, olive leaves, violets, cyclamen, tiny Banksian roses, umbrella-pine needles and cypress sprigs, evocative testimony of the Tuscan countryside's unchanging loveliness.

Emma's wanderlust is part of my inheritance and her herbarium pages combined with a desire to gather first-hand knowledge of the gardens of Renaissance Tuscany took me and my family there for a prolonged visit several years ago. It was love at first sight. It was also a revelation. No matter how many times you read Georgina Masson's excellent text in her book *Italian Gardens*, or study the ground plans in Sir Geoffrey Jellicoe's early work *Italian Gardens of the Renaissance*, nothing quite prepares you for the infinite variety of the Tuscan landscape and the unique character of its gardens, which are derived from the individuality of the cities on which they centre: Lucca, Siena and Florence.

In this book a chapter is devoted to each of the three great cities, and in their introductions I have attempted to give an impression of what strikes me as characterizing these urban centres and the *genius loci* of the gardens in their vicinity.

13

The Tuscan landscape has provided the inspiration for unrivalled feats of creative expression in all the arts, and over the past half millennium these achievements have set the course of Western civilization. That's why there are so many tourists. Florence, Lucca and Siena are choked with people plugging into the Great Art circuit. However, there is more to this heritage than duomos and Ghirlandaio altarpieces. The cool and fragrant hillsides around these great cities are dotted with villas, built by the noble families of the Renaissance as country retreats, where they could retire to escape from the sultry summer heat and the often fatal machinations of court intrigue. And to enhance the serenity of their rural surroundings, they created exquisite gardens where long grassy walks led through shady groves to sunny terraces, perfumed by the scent of citrus flowers from orange and lemon trees set out in huge terracotta pots. The play of water in fountains and cascades provided background music, and still pools laid a carpet of reflected sky at their feet.

A visit to a Tuscan villa garden is one of the best ways I know to see the Italy most visitors miss. In 1903, when Edith Wharton was compiling her book *Italian Villas and Their Gardens*, she grumbled about the difficulty of finding the villas and the discomfort of travelling to them – until she tried the then new motor vehicle. Today, Agriturist organizes bus excursions to some of the private gardens and many of the public ones, but, as Edith found, the best plan is to hire a car. Buy a good map (the regional map produced by Studio F.M.B. Bologna has many of the villas indicated) and take to the open road. Driving along the autostrada from Lucca or Siena to Florence gives you instant understanding of the Italian love of theatre; meandering along a dusty country road affords ample opportunity to appreciate the landscape and study the ingenuity of Italian gardeners.

In even the most basic of homes the garden space is arranged to fulfil all needs: the vine-laden pergola provides restful shade, while flowers and vegetables coexist in unstudied schemes of companion planting. Windowboxes, tubs, containers of every kind are used by town and city dwellers to raise basil, tomatoes, roses, oleander and bay so that even urbanites are party to the beauty of the Italian garden scene.

Many of the finest gardens remain in private hands and the fact that they are open to the public is not broadly advertised so you may well be the only person there. There will be a fee to pay at the gate, and the garden will close for lunch between 12 noon and 2 pm, but otherwise you will be free to enjoy the tranquillity and elegance of the place.

Don't expect to see lavish herbaceous borders and ornamental rose gardens; that type of garden is not geared to the Italian climate. Flowers are used, but primarily in support of the grand design, since villa gardens were conceived as extensions of the house, and the rooms are created by hedges, colonnades and terraces to provide numerous individual areas. Situated on hillsides overlooking distant cities, the *allées* and boundary plantings of the gardens are arranged to accent a panoramic view. Transitions from light to shade, from sun-warmed terrace to cool leafy glade, are what provide movement and interest, and the whole is unified by the repeated use of water. All these elements have been borrowed by designers, from the sixteenth century to the present day, in the creation of gardens throughout Europe and America.

I present this book in the hope that it will display the infinite variety of the Tuscan garden from the grandest to the most humble, from ducal palace to monastic cloister or farmhouse, as a source of inspiration and information for all garden lovers, whether they practise their art in a town or country garden or are one of the growing number of Americans and Northern Europeans who have purchased a Tuscan property and are now wondering how on earth to garden in a Mediterranean climate.

❧ SIENA ❧

In the hills of Chianti, Tuscany's most renowned district, groves of olives and vineyards corrugate the smooth slopes. Olive oil from this region is much prized, being lighter than the robust oils of Lucca, but in 1985 severe frosts killed 90 per cent of the olive trees. Three years later, replanting was well under way with stocks of the four main varieties: Frantoio (the finest olive), Leccino, Moraiolo, and Pendolino (planted in every grove as a pollinator). Harvesting begins in October, and the olives are pulped and pressed within a day or two of picking. Many Chianti *fattorie* market their 'vintage' and varietal oils alongside the wines.

TUSCAN TOWNS were built on hilltops so that they could be more easily defended against the barbarian invasions which surged across the country after the fall of the Roman Empire. But their early inhabitants could not have known that the landscape they were creating, particularly in the area between Florence and Siena, would be one to inspire mankind. In the lowering sun of autumn, the towers of towns like San Gimignano, the walls of Monteriggioni, the rooftops of Radda, glow against the slate sky; capping the hills, their stony structures soften into woodland, vineyard and olive grove. Of all Tuscan hill towns, Siena is generally acknowledged as the most majestic. Dedicated to the Virgin Mary, Queen of Heaven, the city strides three hills, each hill recognized as a *terza* or separate community, but united by the encircling fortifications that snake along the natural contours of the land, and which protect the most perfectly intact medieval city in Tuscany.

Siena owes the preservation of its medieval character to its relative obscurity during the Renaissance period, when the city was a satellite of Medici-dominated Florence. Prior to its subjection by Florence, Siena had, during the twelfth to fourteenth centuries, been one of the most important banking and commercial centres in Europe, achieving this standing despite its being 'all divided and governed more madly than any town in Italy'. Certainly, Siena's early attempts to find a systematic and effective form of government as a republic led to its later instability, exposing it as a suitable target for invasion, insurrection and dictatorship, until the city eventually surrendered its independence in 1555 to the Emperor Charles V. Two years later the city was sold to the Florentines. Cosimo de' Medici set his coat of arms on the face of the Palazzo Pubblico and inaugurated a comparatively peaceful period during which the *castellos* and fortified estates of the Sienese countryside began to adopt some of the refinements of humanism.

Siena's motto, *Cor magis tibi Sena pandit* (Siena opens its heart to you), means that on weekdays and Saturdays, from spring to late autumn, the city is all but unapproachable. Sunday is the day for the independent visitor to appreciate Siena, when it has nothing to offer the dedicated shopper. The artistic and cultural wealth of the city is impressive, and today it is once again besieged, this time by hordes of tourists following the trail of the Sienese Primitive painters who flourished from the late twelfth to the late fourteenth centuries.

A less cerebral, but nonetheless famous attraction is the Palio, a death-defying bare-back horse race run around the Piazza del Campo twice each summer (on 2 July and 16 August). The riders, *gonfaloniere* (standard bearers), drummers, and other attendants are dressed in seventeenth-century costume in the vivid colours of their particular *contrada* (one of several 'parishes' within each *terza*). The horses are marched through the streets to the church of their *contrada*, processing to the beat of drums and the flash of gonfalons as they are hurled and spun skywards by their bearers. Lead weights at the ends of the poles ensure that the banners descend the right way up for faultless catching. To follow behind the *contrade* as they make their way through the narrow streets beneath Siena's graceful Gothic façades conjures the medieval life of the city back into existence.

All streets seem to lead back to the Piazza del Campo, the great open space constructed where the three hills converge. It is spread like a cobblestone cape before the Palazzo Pubblico, and hemmed along its curve with cafes, small restaurants and the broad flights of shallow steps that lead into it. Here one can rest after climbing the Palazzo's Torre del Mangia for a panoramic view of Siena and its surrounds. Sir Harold Acton, in his praise of Siena, astutely observes that the city, an 'outpost of medieval civilization became a model for urban planning when it banned motor traffic from its historic centre. It is a profound satisfaction, even when one is far away, to know that the unique shell-shaped Campo is not used as a parking lot.' Linger in the Campo until the sun begins to fade and then make your way to the cathedral, Siena's other great architectural contribution. Apart from the historical merit of the building and the splendour of the cathedral treasures, an hour's patient study of the play of light on the fabulously ornate fabric, composed of stripes and chevrons of pink, green and white marble, which creates a scene as vivid as the swooping gonfalons of the *contrade*, makes it possible to comprehend the hopes and fears which motivated medieval life.

Later, the Campo becomes the focus for the late evening ritual, the *passaggio*, a pageant of medieval community life, when seemingly all of Siena strolls out after dinner for the evening constitutional in the cool shadows. From tiniest tot to grandmother leaning on her stick, whole families come together in the streets of Siena, all dressed in their best, to see and be seen, meeting neighbours and friends to gossip and dissect the news.

The wooded countryside between Siena and Florence is scattered with castles and fortified villages which offered the only hope of salvation from the brigands and social misfits who plagued the rural communities until well into the eighteenth century. The American writer and novelist, Vernon Lee, who was Edith Wharton's friend and mentor and guided her while she was compiling *Italian Villas and Their Gardens*, described the setting of these bellicose homesteads: 'The plot of ground between the inner and outer rows of wall, where corn and hay might be grown for the horses, is not likely to be given up exclusively to her ladyship's lilies and gillyflowers; salads and roots must grow there, and onions and leeks, for it is not always convenient to get vegetables from the villages below, particularly when there are enemies or disbanded pillaging mercenaries about; hence, also, there will be fewer roses than vines, pears or apples, espaliered against the castle wall.'

In these earliest gardens, decoration was sacrificed for security, and today it appears that their memory has lingered on, so that the gardens of this part of Tuscany are characterized by a more utilitarian or agrarian feeling. Flowers and ornaments are confined to protected corners within the castle walls, *boschi* (wooded groves), if planted, are distant from the dwellings (for in them lurked thieves and murderers). Thus Sienese gardens are more clearly reminiscent of the earliest medieval gardens than the lavish baroqueries of Lucca's palaces and gracious parks or the understated sophistication of the humanistic paradises of the Florentine Renaissance.

The conversion of Siena's medieval castles into the elegant villas modelled on those in the countryside surrounding Florence was almost entirely the work of one man, Baldassare Peruzzi (1481–1536). If the designs for the villas were not actually executed by his own hand, they were certainly influenced by him, as is revealed by their exquisite sense of proportion and scale, which sets Peruzzi's architectural and landscape work (like the graceful farmhouse of L'Apparita (pp. 29–31) apart from all others. Peruzzi's work was only bettered by the younger architect and garden designer, Vignola (1507–1573), who was responsible for the superb garden of Villa Lante at Bagnaia near Rome.

NEAR RADDA

Clinging to the roadside
between Volpaia and Radda,
the walls of an old farmhouse
are set in a foundation of sunny
yellow iris and cerise oxalis,
and will later be shaded by a
grape-vine awning.

PIETRAFITTA

This tiny community, a clutch
of farmhouses around a simple
church, is graced by an opulent
walled garden. Uniformly
clipped box topiary and low
hedges quarter the ground and
provide a formal setting for a
collection of coy nude statuary,
viewed against a backdrop of
the wooded hills of Chianti.
Whoever created this garden
has made a dolls' house version
of the great Medici gardens of
Florence, using – whether
consciously or not – the ancient
formula of a formal garden
framing a distant view of
untamed nature.

CASTELLO DI UZZANO

Attracted by the reputation of this castle's wines and the quality of its olive oil, you discover the beauty of its late 18th-century gardens. When Marion de Jacobert took on their restoration, walls were crumbling and the structure of the planting was blurred. All this has been corrected in the past six years, and the terraces sweep down the gentle slope from the ancient castle walls, past a pair of formal pools, to a *bosco* of cypress and ilex. To reach the garden you must first pass through the *cortile*, a courtyard of cool stone colonnades curtained with trailing ivy.

The parterre is an intriguing mass of cypress clipped to shoulder height and given a pattern by the narrow paths that divide it into geometrical shapes. From this parterre a path, shaded by umbrella pines and hedged with cypress clipped to head height, leads around the garden perimeter to a secret sunken garden.

Throughout the garden at Castello Uzzano the juxtaposition of garden periods and styles is eye-catching. Close to the castle mature specimen trees of blue spruce grow on a terrace decorated with clipped-box topiary cones, topiary edging and this perfectly restored topiary wheel.

Below the evergreen terrace lies the secret sunken garden carpeted with self-sown creeping thyme and sweet alyssum and alive with the buzz of bees and chirrup of grasshoppers singing in the heat of the late afternoon sun. See also p. 2.

CACCHIANO

The English owner of this restored farmhouse utilized the stone-built retaining walls of the vineyard terraces in the creation of a cottage-style garden. Entire terraces are given over to solid plantings of iris and lavender to provide a succession of colour. Beyond lies a mixed-border terrace composed of silver-leafed shrubs such as phlomis, senecio, cistus and sage, interspersed with pink roses.

The terrace is shaded by a wooden pergola covered in tiny-flowered Banksian roses, the ubiquitous climber found in most Tuscan gardens. Unlike many natives, who try to grow plants inappropriate to the Tuscan climate, this transplanted gardener knows the wisdom of suiting plants to the site and so relies entirely on plants that are native to the Mediterranean and southern Europe, and spins out the short flowering periods by planning for a succession of colour.

L'APPARITA
SIENA

Because the garden is made around a farmhouse, its character is essentially informal, although the areas most easily seen from the approach road and through which you pass to reach the flower garden are more disciplined and devoted to evergreen shrubs planted in a formal manner. To one side of the house an avenue of pleached ilex is taking shape, reminiscent of the 'Stilt' garden at Hidcote Manor in Gloucestershire. These clipped-box balls in terracotta urns give sculptural interest to an expanse of grass.

Designed in 1960 by Italy's greatest modern landscape designer, Pietro Porcinai, the gardens surrounding the simple farmhouse serve as a stage setting for the spectacular view of distant Siena, and as a theatre for international stars of the opera who are frequent house guests of the owner. The farmhouse is all that remains of a larger structure, and is recognized as being one of the earliest works of Baldassare Peruzzi (1481–1536), who had a hand in many of the great villas surrounding Siena, including Celsa and Vicobello. Observing the simple origins of L'Apparita, Porcinai created a garden that is nearly indistinguishable from the surrounding natural landscape, using only native trees and shrubs to enhance the illusion of a garden that is not a garden.

The glory of the garden is the view of Siena, which has been framed in such a way that it is unblemished by any suggestion of the 20th century: cypress, ilex and numerous deciduous trees have been positioned to screen the more obvious distant eyesores, and the natural terrain has been sculpted into gentle banks and berms to conceal nearby roads and buildings. Even the drive up to the villa's parking area is sunk into a man-made ravine, the banks of which are planted with gorse and berberis. From this area, the lowest level in the garden, you ascend through a dark tunnel walled with cotoneaster into brightness at the house entrance. The doorway is framed in a collar of dark green ivy that can be studded with fruit and flowers to make a living garland at times of special celebration.

The gardens Porcinai created were each as unique and individual as the site and the client, but were all influenced by his advocacy of the ecological garden, a cause he championed long before it became fashionable. He shared the Renaissance belief that it is imperative for mankind to live in harmony with the natural world and the earth which sustains us. That this credo directed his work can be most readily seen at L'Apparita, where, although the feats of landscape engineering were prodigious, the finished garden is one of breathtaking simplicity, seeming not to have been constructed at all. The undulations of its lawns and the sparseness of the planting echo the contours of the distant hills of the region of southern Tuscany known as Le Crete.

PIENZA

A medieval village transformed into a model of Renaissance city planning by the architect Bernardo Rossellino for his client Pope Pius II, Pienza was 'born of a tender feeling of love and a dream of beauty'. Radiating from the cathedral square, the narrow cobbled streets are densely built-up, the elevations of dignified palaces, chapels, civic buildings and simple family dwellings hemming in the tiny public squares and pavements. Consequently, gardening space is at a premium in the old town, so potted plants are lined up to make container-grown borders, in this case of aspidistra and arum lilies, to soften the sombre stonework.

Jasminum mesnyi shades a house entrance and a collection of potted plants, including clivia, aspidistra and gardenias. The warm, humid microclimate, created by heat released from the sun-baked stone walls and the moisture of early-morning watering, helps container-grown gardens such as this to flourish in the streets of Pienza.

PALAZZO PICCOLOMINI
PIENZA

This elegant palace, located next to the cathedral, is Rossellino's finest building. From the street it has all the stature of his Palazzo Rucellai in Florence, but the garden side is a triple loggia, vying in grace and beauty with the magnificent panorama of the Val d'Orcia over which it looks. You enter the palace *cortile* and directly opposite is the entrance to a perfectly preserved *Quattrocento* garden; only the fountain set at the circular intersection of the paths is relatively new. This simple garden room, filled with the scent of box and alive with birdsong and the chirrup of grasshoppers, acts as a foil to the splendour of the palace and the majesty of the distant landscape, and exemplifies the Renaissance architect Alberti's dictates on the making of gardens (see p. 63).

ORTI LEONINI
SAN QUIRICO D'ORCIA

In the 12th century this small town southeast of Siena was a stronghold of the Emperor Frederick Barbarossa. Below the fortress ruins and those of Torre del Cassero lie all that remains of a 16th-century formal garden, used today, as it was in the past, as a public park. On two sides the parterre is bordered by arbours of ilex, and on the third side, which is the slope of the mound that elevates the fortress, ilex grows to make a shady grove. The web of string stretched across the garden above the lines of box is there to guide the gardeners as they clip the hedges, helping them to maintain uniform height and width.

❧ LUCCA ❧

VILLA GARZONI
COLLODI

Villa Garzoni was built at a time when Rome was gaining the upper hand politically and artistically throughout Italy, and the layout of the garden is more derivative of the grandiose Villa d'Este at Tivoli than of the simple charm of the Villa Medici at Fiesole. The architectural treatment of the hillside, with its single axis of massive staircases and sequence of pools and terraces, treats the garden as a single unit devolving from formality into informality, rather than as a series of small formal compositions or garden rooms that revolve in unison around the villa. As an example of the Baroque it is hard to equal, but equally hard to take. See also p. 53.

HILAIRE BELLOC described Lucca as the 'neatest, the regularest, the exactest, the most fly-in-amber little town in the world, with its uncrowded streets, its absurd fortifications, and its contented silent houses – all like a family at ease and at rest under the sun'.

It is rather unjust to call Lucca's mighty walls absurd fortifications, for they are what have preserved the city's unique character through centuries of change, and in the modern age have contributed largely to its substance. Approaching Lucca from the main Pisa–Florence road through small villages and the Lucchese suburban sprawl, the walls rise up in sudden splendour from the surrounding river plain. Today smooth grass lawns replace the original wide water-filled moat, and lime trees, magnificent in their maturity, take the place of soldiers on the ramparts. Nothing of the antique city can be seen, and you gyrate wildly round the ring road before drawing a sharp breath and plunging through one of the gates – and back in time.

To the Romans, Lucca was even more important than Florence, which had been created by Julius Caesar as a convenient river crossing. At Lucca, in 60 BC, Caesar formed the First Triumvirate with Pompey and Crassus. He built the first walls, laid out the streets within according to the Roman sense of ordered uniformity and built the amphitheatre.

All of these things were preserved by following generations. The limestone Roman walls form the foundations for the present walls of brick-faced masonry; work on them began in 1594 and was completed one hundred and fifty years later. The streets within preserve their gridiron pattern and open onto piazzas dominated by churches, the architecture of which is as unique as the city itself. The two most imposing are the twelfth-century Romanesque San Michele and the largely thirteenth-century cathedral dedicated to San Martino. Both possess galleried façades superimposed on simple brick

37

structures – ornate palisades of thin marble columns, carved with fantastic animals, human forms, simple geometric shapes or inlaid with coloured stone, each one different from its neighbours. Of the two, San Michele is the most startling: four layers of ornamented limestone columns are crowned by Saint Michael killing a dragon. The solidity of the figure is curiously at odds with the fragility of the colonnades below and the free-standing appearance of the façade (there was not enough money to finish the church so its roofline reaches only part of the way up the façade).

San Martino is only marginally less fantastic, but, as if to compensate, the north transept is graced with the 1406 tomb effigy of Ilaria del Carretto, the inspired masterpiece of the otherwise unremarkable Jacopo della Quercia. Few images rival the eloquence and touching sadness of this young woman's peaceful visage.

The Piazza dell' Anfiteatro, which is also the marketplace, was created from the remains of the Roman amphitheatre. Lucca held its own against rival Tuscan cities throughout the Dark Ages, being consecutively the stronghold of Goths, Lombards and Franks, until the eleventh century when the latter moved their Tuscan powerbase to Florence. In 1808 Tuscany was annexed to the French Empire and governed by Napoleon's sister Elisa who was made Grand Duchess. Lucca was where she established her court, settling at the Villa Reale, at Marlia, a few miles north of the city.

Lucca's role as a prominent political centre brought its old villas and gardens into the limelight of fashion, where they were subsequently found lacking. Thus, more than most, the gardens in the vicinity of Lucca suffered from the early nineteenth-century vogue for transforming the old-fashioned formal gardens of pools, fountains and parterres into 'naturalized' English-style landscape parks. Sir Reginald Blomfield, the architect and author of *The Formal Garden in England*, whose work was influential in popularizing the Italianate garden in England during the late-Victorian and Edwardian periods, wrote 'that in the one instance in which English taste in a matter of design has taken hold on the Continent, it has done so with such disastrous results'. So we today must mourn the loss of the formal gardens of Villa Mansi, be grateful for what remains of Flora's garden at the Villa Torrigiani, and ignore the modern 'touches' at Villa Garzoni to understand what the splendour of Lucca's Baroque gardens must once have been.

Lucca had maintained its independence during the struggles for supremacy between the great Tuscan city-states which occupied much of the late medieval period, and occupations by the French and the Austrians during the eighteenth and nineteenth centuries only further consolidated Lucca's position as a sovereign city. Not until Lucca became part of the Grand Duchy of Tuscany in 1847 and part of the Kingdom of Italy in 1861, did it throw in its lot with its neighbours. This heritage of independence and position as a 'royal domain' may go some way to explaining the highly individualistic style of its stately villas and gardens, which are far more ostentatious than those of homely Florence or defensive Siena. It is also reflected in the character of the city and its inhabitants, who, while graciously accepting the attentions of tourists, do not appear to court them actively – Lucca sits serenely on the outskirts of the frantic itinerary of most tourists in Italy.

That, however, was not always the case. In the 1580s, the French essayist Montaigne visited the Bagni di Lucca, a spa due north of the city that was, and still is, renowned for its health-giving waters. Shelley and Mary Godwin took a house in the chestnut forests near the spa and returned to nature in an effort to improve the poet's health. The Tennysons thought to do likewise on the recommendation of Robert Browning, but their stay was not a success, as they wouldn't eat the food but the mosquitoes would eat them.

Perhaps the most profound effect that Lucca had on any tourist, the reverberations of which were to redraw the perimeters of English architecture and landscape design, was the one experienced by John Ruskin (1819–1900). In his words, 'suddenly in the presence of twelfth-century buildings, originally set in such balance of masonry that they could all stand without mortar; and in material so incorruptible, that after six hundred years of sunshine and rain a lancet could not now be put between their joints. . . . Absolutely for the first time I now saw what medieval builders were and what they meant . . . and thereon literally *began* the study of architecture.'

Montaigne described the scenery around Lucca thus: 'all about the cornfields are rows of trees, each tree being attached to its neighbour by vines, wherefore these fields have all the appearance of gardens.' Three hundred years later that is still very much the case, but many of the fields and vines have been replaced by *vivai*, or nursery gardens. It is an awesome sight to see row upon row of *Magnolia grandiflora*, varying in size from the merest maiden to a specimen 15 feet tall, or ranks of *Cupressus sempervirens*, the characteristic evergreen column of the Tuscan countryside, alternating with groves of umbrella pines and more ornamental evergreens than you could shake a stick at. From Lucca to Pistoia each side of the road is festooned with flocks of ornamental trees and shrubs or blanketed with polythene tunnels, under which shelter crops of carnations, gazanias, chrysanthemums, irises, long-stemmed roses, and every cut-flower imaginable, changing with the seasons to supply the central Tuscan flower market at Pistoia.

Scattered among all this horticultural industry are the olive groves and sunflower fields, cultivated to supply the oil-producing industry for which Lucca is famous, and the homely *orti di famiglia*, or kitchen gardens, with their carefully nurtured crops of tomatoes, onions, garlic, chards, salad greens and countless other fruits and vegetables for the family table.

PIAZZA SAN
GIOVANNI
LUCCA

Behind the high walls that surround many Lucchese houses lie gardens created in a manner called *pensile*, gardens that are elevated above ground level, either by filling in the courtyard with soil, or by making an earth-covered terrace. This traditional *giardino pensile* (built up 12 to 15 feet above ground level) is attached to a 17th-century priest's house next to the church of San Giovanni. Four generations of one family have made it into a tranquil secret garden, planted with plum, peach, olive and magnolia trees, underplanted with crocuses and daffodils, followed by irises, roses and lilies to mark the season's change. A fountain above the old well provides refreshing music, and a wistaria-covered pergola caps the wall of a loggia overlooking the street.

PIAZZA DEL
MERCATO
LUCCA

Built in 1834 by decree of Leopold II on the site of a Roman amphitheatre, this is an early example of public housing. The plain functionality of the buildings surrounding the cobbled marketplace is enlivened by dressed-up balconies draped with trailing pelargoniums, and stands of houseplants. Agave, aucuba, tradescantia, scented geraniums, aeoniums, arums and myriad others take the air and sun.

VILLA MANSI
SEGROMIGNO

The villa was originally a *Cinquecento* building but was extensively remodelled in the mid-1660s. The gardens, laid out over seven years from 1725, included formal box-edged flowerbeds, fountains, an ornamental fishpond and the legendary Bath of Diana. The last two features are all that remain after the gardens were levelled by the 'Englishing' of the landscape in the 1880s, when the formal beds were replaced by sweeping lawns and an extensive park.

Water, abundant in this area, provided the wherewithal for the charming water gardens of the Lucchese countryside; it was also, according to legend, the source of the everlasting beauty of one of the villa's early owners, Lucida Mansi. She is said to have made a pact with the Devil to preserve her looks, provided she bathed in a tranquil pool each day – hence the Bath of Diana. She bathes here still, supposedly, having met her end in the garden, felled by a stroke of lightning during a thunderstorm.

Creamy white bracts blanket a fine specimen tree of *Cornus kousa chinensis* in the Elysian gardens of the Villa Mansi. While some may regret the loss of the original 17th-century gardens that surrounded the Mannerist villas in the hills surrounding Lucca, the English-style landscape gardens which replaced them are more successful here than in other parts of Italy, where the climate is drier and water less available to nourish lawns and parks.

In the landscaped park, paths slice through cool evergreen bowers of ilex and bay, which frame vistas of fine sculpture and enhance the romanticism of the setting.

VILLA TORRIGIANI
CAMIGLIANO

Sir Harold Acton, in explaining how the villa we see today is a mid-17th-century make-over of an earlier, less ornate building, describes how the façade looks 'as if an intricate mask had been clapped on to a simpler frame – a mask of varied materials and tints. Lions on the steps, niches containing busts over the flanking statues, carved plaques, sculptured coats of arms, and squadrons of statues . . .'. This Mannerist confection, when skirted by its original formal parterres, must have given cause for a sharp intake of breath. Even today, surrounded by a more tranquil landscape of sweeping lawns and romantic groves of specimen trees, Torrigiani retains its flamboyance.

The original formal gardens vanished in the 19th century when the vogue for landscaped parks in the English style had the owners of old Renaissance gardens by the throat. All that survived was the spectacular Garden of Flora, a sunken garden with the Grotto of the Seven Winds at one end and this elegant double staircase at the other. What probably saved this garden from destruction was that it was in fact an enormous *gioco d'acqua*, or water joke, a sort of architectural squirt-gun, which had been a popular feature in Italian gardens since Roman times.

Water from this reservoir, located in the *bosco* above the sunken garden and decorated with fountains, statuary and pot-grown citrus, feeds the *giochi* embedded in the steps and balustrades of the staircase leading to Flora's garden.

As you approach the balustrade to look down over the flowerbeds, a tap hidden in a grotto below the staircase is turned on to activate jets of water that spout from the steps, chasing you down the stairs and along the central path through the garden until eventually you arrive at the Grotto of the Seven Winds. Much of the lead piping which fed the jets in the garden path was stolen or damaged during the Second World War, but Principe Torrigiani is financing the restoration of these and other non-working sections of the *giochi*.

Refuge is sought inside the grotto, which is decorated with stone mosaic, tufa stone or *spugna* work, false stalactites and marble statues of the winds. The current of air created by the water running through the plumbing to the *giochi* is vented at the mouths of the marble figures. More jets of water shoot up from the floor and the *coup de grâce* is delivered by Flora herself, who, from her perch on top of the cupola, pours forth a torrent of water into the centre of the grotto, drenching anyone foolish enough to seek safety in its depths.

The retaining wall of the double staircase in Flora's garden is set with fountains which sadly no longer play their streams into the shell basins beneath the grimacing masks. But a little imagination employed when the staircase is alive with water jets brings back the original gaiety of the scene.

Outside the precincts of Flora's sunken garden a small parterre of box graces the terrace before the summerhouse. Under its windows, against the south-facing wall, a verdant hedge of lemon-scented verbena, *Lippia citriodora*, fills the garden with perfume when warmed by the sun's rays.

VILLA GARZONI
COLLODI

Few of Tuscany's great gardens are owned by the *comune* in which they are located. This one is, and its proximity to the Pinocchio theme park may explain its over-exuberant planting of outlandish topiary and blinding formal bedding. However, it is Baroque, dating largely from the second half of the 17th century. The gardens are laid out on a hillside beside the villa, rather than behind as is usual. Above the formal parterre is a terraced grove of ilex bisected by a vast water cascade flowing from a unique bath house at the top of the hill. This was intended for social gatherings rather than for personal hygiene, and was converted from an early 17th-century hermitage, where lived a hermit employed to stroll around the gardens. See also p. 36.

VILLA BRUGHIERE
CAMIGLIANO

The proximity of the mountains in this area, providing a ready supply of water, made it comparatively easy to create villa gardens that made a feature of fountains and pools. Notable examples are Villa Reale at Marlia, Villa Torrigiani, and this elegant 17th-century villa. While all of the formal gardens here have been replaced by lawns and groves of specimen trees, the circular pools and grotto remain. This is the north-facing back of the villa. The circular pool is twinned with another pool before the south-facing front, which is flanked by a pair of fountains, the water course terminating at the main gate in an overgrown grotto.

The water is brought to the garden from the mountains, beyond which lies the spa of Bagni di Lucca. It enters the garden at this series of stepped pools, flows underground to the circular pool at the back of the villa, passes underneath the foundations and then emerges at the grand formal pool and fountains at the villa's entrance.

The abundance of water contributes to the vigour of the kitchen garden in front of Villa Brughiere's *limonaia* (lemon house). The vivid red of ripe plum tomatoes grown on cane tepees and the solid grey of artichokes and cardoons add colour and architectural interest to the rows of chard, chicory, *fagioli* (beans) and sweet-scented rosemary. The Tuscan gardener takes as much pride in the presentation of the vegetable garden as of the ornamental garden.

VINCI

At the end of April, on the slopes below Leonardo da Vinci's birthplace, a blanket of poppies is spread beneath the aged boughs of grey-green olive trees. In late June, the ochre-coloured soil complements the turquoise residue of copper sulphate sprayed on vines and tomatoes. Natural, uncontrived colour harmonies like this abound in the Tuscan countryside, and are as worth noting as anything seen in formal gardens elsewhere in Europe, Italy or England, where colour schemes are studiously, and not always successfully, erected.

❦ FLORENCE ❦

VILLA GAMBERAIA
SETTIGNANO

Of the many villas and gardens located on the hillsides surrounding Florence, none is more loved than that of Gamberaia, which began life in the 15th century as a simple farmhouse. The gardens were begun in 1717, and although minor changes have been made over the centuries the original plan is unaltered. Edith Wharton, writing in 1904, said the gardens were 'the most perfect example of the art of producing great effect on a small scale'. Fifty years later, Georgina Masson remarked that they were the 'loveliest and most typically Tuscan' that she had seen, and more recently Sir Harold Acton described Gamberaia as 'a most poetical garden – a jewel'. See also pp. 96–103.

'Cerchi chi vuol le pompe e gli altri onori . . .' 'Let those who want to seek pomp and glory . . . and the rewards that are accompanied by a thousand disturbing thoughts and a thousand sadnesses. A green meadow full of lovely flowers, a stream that washes its grassy banks, a little bird that sings of love are more satisfying to our desires. The leafy woods, the rocks, high hills, and dark caves . . . bring love's bright eyes to life before me. [In the city] one thing after another deprives me of them.'

WHEN LÒRENZO DE' MEDICI wrote his little verse extolling the virtue of simple country pleasures in preference to the angst of life in the town, he was effectively eulogizing the rustic nature of the villas and gardens of the Florentine Renaissance, a quality which sets them apart from those of courtly Lucca and feudal Siena.

Florence was the birthplace of the Renaissance. The closing years of the *Trecento* saw the city consolidating its dominance over other Tuscan cities, and in 1419, with the end of schism in the Catholic Church, Pope Martin V chose Florence to house St Peter's keys. From the early 1400s, the city's pre-eminence attracted scholars and artists from all over Europe. Here they received generous patronage from the Florentine nobility. Families such as Albizzi, Strozzi, Uzzano and the up-and-coming Medici encouraged the development of the arts and humanities while engaging in some rigorous jockeying for absolute control of Florence – the Medici pitted against nearly everyone else.

The founder of the mightiest Florentine dynasty was Giovanni de' Medici, who was the richest banker in Italy during the early fifteenth century. But it was his son Cosimo who brought the Medici to the top of the heap, which he accomplished with little regard for the niceties of life. His maxims were: 'Better a city ruined than a city lost', and 'New and worthy citizens can be made by a few ells of crimson cloth'. Cosimo crushed the noble families which opposed him, bankrupting them with fines and taxes or simply by forcing them into exile, and replaced them with other families (of lesser ability) whose loyalty he bought by bestowing honour and wealth. Cosimo was ruthless, but not particularly bloodthirsty, although not above arranging a murder to further his family's ends.

There was another, possibly redeeming, side to Cosimo's despotic nature, for his private life was conducted simply and without the tendency to ostentation which is normally manifest in absolute tyrants. He was a devoted family man and preferred leading the life of a country squire at his rural retreats – Il Trebbio in the Mugello, north of Florence, or the villas at Careggi or Cafaggiolo – to living in his city palazzo. Even there Cosimo exercised restraint, for it was a plain square unadorned building. He disliked any kind of show, and valued modesty above all other personal qualities; the only displays he actively encouraged were the cultural pyrotechnics of the artists and scholars he patronized. Fra Filippo Lippi, Michelozzo, Donatello, Brunelleschi were just a few of the great Renaissance stars supported by Cosimo, and many of Florence's finest early Renaissance buildings were erected through his benefaction.

It is rather sad that Cosimo's generosity was not entirely altruistic. His friend and biographer, Vespasiano da Bisticci, wrote: 'He did these things because it appeared to him that he held money, not over well acquired . . . .' However, Cosimo realized that the nature of his fellow citizens was such that the Medici could vanish without a trace in the space of a generation, but the buildings and artworks would remain to ensure the family's immortality.

Lorenzo the Magnificent, Cosimo's grandson, was the next family member to leave a significant mark on Florence, assuming power in 1469, at the age of twenty-one. Like his grandfather, the ruthlessness of his inner nature, which turned him into a despot, was mantled by his outward show of sensitivity; for Lorenzo was also a patron of the arts, a confirmed aesthete whose principles were laced with a healthy dose of hedonism. Of Lorenzo it has been said that 'Florence could not have had a better or more delightful tyrant.' When Cosimo came to power, the golden sun of the Renaissance had begun its rise; under Lorenzo it reached its full ascendency. The *Quattrocento* remains one of history's most glorious epochs. From Florence, and under the auspices of the Medici and wealthy bourgeoisie, the civilizing influence of the Renaissance spread over the rest of Europe, informing every aspect of creative life, from the artist at his easel to the garden designer laying out the pleasure grounds around an English manor house.

However, Florence did not long remain the intellectual hub of Europe. Two years after Lorenzo's death in 1492, the first invasions of Italy by alien powers began, and these relentless conflicts were to undermine the stability of the country until the end of the nineteenth century. Nevertheless, Florence and its citizens have over the centuries retained many of the qualities which were ingrained by the attitudes of the Medici and the classically inspired ideas of the Renaissance. The city and its people are understated but possessed of great style, proud yet modest, gracious and disinclined to any outward show of emotion or temper, to the degree of seeming arrogant. These qualities are reflected in the gardens and villas which stud the necklace of hills surrounding the city – in the Mugello, at Fiesole and Settignano. Scratch a sophisticated Florentine and you will find a *paesano* not very far below the surface, and just as the farmer works with his land, so the wealthy villa owners, employing architects like Giorgio Vasari in the sixteenth century or Pietro Porcinai in the twentieth, created gardens that gently manipulated the countryside rather than dominating it.

The reactions of visitors to Florence over the years have been mixed. In the eighteenth century the writer Stendhal suffered the first attack of the affliction which today bears his name; tourists usually succumb to the 'Stendhals' when they're overcome by the beauty and splendour of what they've seen. Transported by 'the very notion of being in Florence', he wrote, 'the tide of emotion . . . flowed so deep that it scarce was to be distinguished from religious awe . . . I was seized with a fierce palpitation of the heart; I walked in constant fear of falling to the ground.' Mark Twain, however, was not so impressed, least of all by the Arno: 'It is popular to admire the Arno . . . they [the Florentines] call it a river, and they honestly think it a river . . . They even help out the delusion by building bridges over it. I do not see why they are too good to wade.' But then he was comparing it to the Mississippi.

Florence has drawn expatriates like moths to a candle, particularly English and Americans. Yet the natives still profess, in all modesty, of course, not to understand the phenomenon. They find it mildly entertaining, for example, that anyone would want to take pictures of their gardens. No doubt this has something to do with their innate reserve, but also because the city and its environs have so much to offer that has always been there, that the Florentines take it for granted. Yet we come to marvel and wallow in their heritage, hoping that some of its greatness will rub off on us.

The villa gardens of Fiesole and Settignano, and similar villages surrounding Florence, were the chief source of inspiration to English and American garden designers during the early part of this century. Norah Lindsay and Lawrence Johnston, Vita Sackville-West, Harold Peto, Thomas Mawson, Edwin Lutyens and countless others made the Florentine pilgrimage and brought home visions of enclosed garden rooms, pergola-covered walks, long avenues ending in distant views, formal parterres of clipped box and landmark plantings of ilex and cypress. Others stayed and created their gardens or res-

GIARDINO TORRIGIANI
FLORENCE

The guide to this garden, published in 1824 soon after it was completed, lists no fewer than thirty-one separate garden features including a Gothic-style basilica, Merlin's grotto, a botanical garden dedicated to Linnaeus, a sacred wood and sepulchre, an aviary and numerous fountains, cascades and *giochi d'acqua*. It was created by Marchese Pietro Torrigiani at the same time as his brother was transforming the gardens of the Villa Torrigiani near Lucca into a romantic English-style park. See also pp. 144–5.

tored those which were derelict. The notable art historian Bernard Berenson and his wife Mary made their home, I Tatti, into a cultural centre, attracting the literary and artistic 'glitterati' of the time to their gracefully renovated villa, which was surrounded by an idealized recreation of an old Tuscan garden. Their guests included the American writer Edith Wharton, whose book *Italian Gardens and Their Villas* was one of the first on the subject this century and brought the gardens of Tuscany to an appreciative audience in the United States and England.

The garden of I Tatti was designed by a young English architect, Cecil Pinsent (1884–1964). He was to establish his reputation in Tuscany, remodelling villas and designing gardens for the expatriate community centred on Florence. Pinsent was exceptionally sensitive to landscape and had a sound knowledge of Renaissance design. Sir Geoffrey Jellicoe recalls that in 1923 he spent a day in Fiesole with Pinsent, who he came to regard as his first 'maestro' in the art of placing buildings in the landscape. The gardens of I Tatti and Le Balze are adequate testimony to Pinsent's talent, the buildings and gardens complementing each other perfectly and uniting sympathetically with the surrounding landscape. This style of garden, which is particularly Tuscan, was influenced by the writing of Leon Battista Alberti, the first architect of the early Renaissance to incorporate the classical orders in a building, and the author of *De Re Aedificatoria*, written around the middle of the fifteenth century. In it Alberti consistently referred to the 'ancients', advocating a return to the design practices of classical Rome, particularly in the planning and planting of gardens.

Alberti specifically recommended that villas and their gardens be sited on hillsides so that they commanded excellent views that would 'overlook the city, the owner's land, the sea or a great plain and familiar hills and mountains', views which would then be 'framed by a delicacy of gardens'. The gardens, and likewise the villas and their inhabitants, would benefit from the exposure to health-giving breezes and sunshine of a hillside site.

His dependence on the garden design of ancient Rome was evident, for he held that box should be clipped into low hedges to make decorative patterns, and flowering and fruiting trees should be grown in pots and used to border paths through the garden. Urns and pots of every description should be filled with flowers and placed around the garden to add variety of colour and shape. Marble-pillared pergolas garlanded with roses and grapes should provide shady retreats, as would small groves of cypress, ilex (*Quercus ilex* or evergreen oak), bay and myrtle. Water, either in pools or gushing from fountains, should be everywhere in the garden for the refreshing sound of its music. Long grass avenues as were popular in medieval gardens should be included to provide space for gentle sporting pastimes such as bowls.

PALAZZO CORSINI
SUL PRATO
FLORENCE

Safe inside the shelter of a *limonaia*, orange and lemon trees wait out the winter. The tall south-facing windows admit the maximum light so that the trees continue to photosynthesize and the fruit to ripen. In the spring they will once again be set around the garden on their individual stone plinths, each one numbered to resume its correct place.

Grottoes were an important feature, in his opinion, and should be constructed 'as the ancients used to do, covering the surface with rough and rocky things, putting there little bits of pumice, spongy stone and travertine'. He also approved of shell decoration.

However, the idea of the areas of a garden being organized into a symmetrical arrangement along a central axis did not come from Alberti. The earliest known plan including such a scheme is by Baldassare Peruzzi (see p. 19) in a garden design drawn at the beginning of the sixteenth century. Until that time, garden 'rooms' did not have separate existences and bore no spatial relationship to one another.

This then was the platform upon which Tuscan garden design was erected, and one has only to look at gardens such as Villa Gamberaia, I Tatti and Le Balze to understand the impact of the Renaissance ideal on twentieth-century landscape design in England, Europe and America.

VILLA MEDICI
FIESOLE

This was the first true Renaissance villa and garden, built for Cosimo de' Medici by Michelozzo Michelozzi, *c*. 1458–61, and was later Lorenzo the Magnificent's favourite 'rural' retreat, where he entertained the philosophers, poets and artists under his patronage. It remained in the Medici family until 1671, and was eventually sold in 1772 to the controversial Lady Orford, Horace Walpole's sister-in-law. In the 19th century, it was owned by the artist William Blundell Spence and then, in 1911, was acquired by Lady Sybil Cutting, whose second husband was the writer Geoffrey Scott. The garden had been altered considerably over the centuries, but Scott's partner, the architect Cecil Pinsent, restored much of its Renaissance character.

Positioned on a steep hillside the garden consists of two main terraces, that in front of the villa serving as an extension of the villa's main rooms, with a grassy bowling green set slightly above it against the hillside boundary. The lower terrace, reached by a subterranean passage, was used as a promenade. From these terraces, the spectacular views over Florence and the valley of the Arno can be enjoyed, and while the planting is Pinsent's 20th-century interpretation of the *Cinquecento* style, the layout of the garden is substantially original, and perfectly illustrates Alberti's maxim that a garden should frame a distant view and be open to health-giving breezes. A ramp leads from the lower terrace to the back of the villa where the *giardino segreto*, secret garden, is found.

A pergola-covered arcade built against the retaining wall of the upper terrace provides a vantage point from which to view the formal parterre below, which is planted with box-edged flowerbeds and conical *Magnolia grandiflora*. Beyond this well-ordered environment were the fields and olive groves of the neighbouring farms. Lady Sybil's daughter, Marchesa Iris Origo (whose own garden at La Foce was designed by Cecil Pinsent), recalled the fragrances and flowers of the hillside *podere* (farm), and also remarked on the English inclination to introduce a misplaced note of home, planting 'Dorothy Perkins' roses and wistaria on the pergolas of their Italian villa gardens.

The least altered area of the garden is the tiny *giardino segreto* behind the villa. It is a simple space, shaded by magnolia and divided into grassy box-edged quarters, and otherwise unadorned except for a pool and fountain that plays with a single jet. Yet in all the garden, it commands the finest view of Florence, to be enjoyed from a corner where the wall is broken by a balustrade. Thus quiet contemplation and appreciation of the magnificent view are undisturbed by the nearness of the garden designer's art. Across the road which runs below the garden wall lies Le Balze, another Cecil Pinsent garden, whose cypress walks and topiary can just be discerned.

VILLA MEDICI
CASTELLO

Designed by Niccolò Tribolo for Cosimo I, work on the villa began in 1538 and was completed after Tribolo's death by Buontalenti and Amannati. The garden was intended as an iconological celebration of the power of the Medici family, and became Cosimo's retirement home, where he devoted his old age to the cultivation of a particular strain of jasmine, the *Mugherino del Granduca o di Goa (Jasminum sambac goensis)*. The main garden is a square walled enclosure sited on a gentle slope behind the villa, which more nearly resembles a medieval enclosed garden – as does that of Palazzo Piccolomini (p. 34) – than the outward-looking Medici garden at Fiesole. At one time the central fountain was further enclosed by a *cabinet de verdure* of clipped cypress.

The change of level between the lower slope and the upper terraces is marked by an ornate grotto, one of the main features of the central axis. Decorated with mosaics, fountains (at one time water would have spouted from the animals' mouths and birds' beaks) and *giochi d'acqua*, the sculptures represent the rivers Arno and Mugnone, thus signifying the greatness of the Medici.

Grottoes and fountains in many Tuscan gardens are decorated with shell, pebble and tufa-stone mosaics, such as this composition on the ceiling of the grotto at Castello, their intricacy adding to the opulence of the gardens.

On the uppermost terrace an ilex *bosco* or labyrinth shelters the fountain of Janus by the sculptor Ammannati. To either side of the main garden were small enclosed secret gardens, one of which in Cosimo's time contained a tree house, its walls fashioned from trained branches, reached by an ivy-clad staircase that had water jets hidden in its foliage-covered treads. The garden on the other side was a formal herb garden which, according to Vasari, was given over to the cultivation of 'strange and medicinal herbs'.

I COLLAZZI
NEAR FLORENCE

Tradition has it that this magnificent villa on the via Volterrana was designed by Michelangelo, since he was a friend of Agostino Dino for whom it was built in 1560. The grandeur of the building and the countryside surrounding it precludes the need or desire for ornate gardens, so that it is only on the terrace below the retaining wall, reached via a sunken staircase let into the path in front of the villa, that a parterre garden is discovered. Elsewhere simplicity prevails. A stately cypress avenue leading to the villa separates two grassy terraces. The upper one is thickly planted with ilex and oak around a reservoir that feeds water to the more formal pool on the terrace below, which reflects the villa in its mirror-like sheet of water. Heavily damaged by shelling in 1944, I Collazzi has been beautifully restored by the Marchi family, who also own Villa Gamberaia. See also p. 1.

PARCO DEMIDOFF
PRATOLINO

Work on this garden, designed by Buontalenti for Francesco de' Medici and formerly known as the Pratolino, began in about 1569. By the end of the century it was renowned throughout Europe for the splendour of its automata, cascades, fountains and *giochi d'acqua*, which rivalled even the lavish displays of the Villa d'Este at Tivoli. By 1814 the garden was nearly derelict, and the Austrian Archduke Ferdinand III converted it to a *giardino inglese*. But this colossal statue, L'Appennino, remains. Attributed to Giambologna, the god Apennine bears down his great weight on the head of a monster, causing a torrent of water to issue from its mouth into the huge basin that once crowned the amphitheatre behind the villa.

PETRAIA
CASTELLO

In 1364 the castle of Petraia withstood an attack by mercenaries led by the English knight Sir John Hawkwood, but in 1575 it was put to more gentle use and converted by Buontalenti for Cardinal Ferdinando de' Medici into a palatial villa surrounded by graceful gardens equalling those of nearby Villa Medici, Castello. However, its design is completely unlike that of its sister. Situated high on a hill overlooking the Arno valley, the gardens are laid out below the villa, the ribbons of box-edged beds appearing like a chenille blanket.

The terrace between the villa level and the parterre is taken up by a vast rectangular pool filled with giant carp, the uniform surface of the water providing a contrast to the textures and patterns of the garden and vista beyond. The novelist Elizabeth Sewell described the garden in 1871: 'a dream of beauty it is; – terraces bordered by trellis-work, and orange trees, with showers of roses, magnolias and azaleas; a view over Florence and away to the Carrara mountains; and behind the villa, a hill, planted with trees, commanding another view in a different direction and having at its base one of those broad solemn cypress avenues which form the contrast wanting to set off the glory of an Italian sky.'

GIARDINO DI BOBOLI
FLORENCE

This is the most famous Medicean garden and as unlike the others as chalk and cheese, for this was the regal garden of the Palazzo Pitti, designed for lavish displays of state. Begun in 1549 and enlarged and improved over the centuries, its layout was governed by the natural terrrain. It stretches southwards towards the Porta Romana along a wide cypress avenue that forms a cross axis and leads to the Piazzale dell' Isolotto (shown here), designed by Alfonso Parigi. This island in a circular pool is reached via footbridges, and the central fountain is surmounted by an enormous statue of Oceano – Giambologna's original statue is now in the Bargello Palace.

The Boboli Gardens as we see them today follow much the same plan as was established by the end of the 17th century. By that time the original garden scheme, which was based on the Tuscan principle of controlled siting and planting, had given way to the Roman idea of strong architectural treatment for a landscape. Baccio Bandinelli, who worked for the Medici, wrote to Cosimo I: *'Che cose che si murano debbono essere guidi e superiori a quelle che si piantono'* (The things which are built should dominate and be the guide of those which are planted). The various parts of the Boboli Gardens are linked by arbours of ilex, now grown to great size, and their depths provide shady relief from the vast open areas of the garden, which on a sunny day are almost too hot to enjoy.

GIARDINO DELLE ROSE
FLORENCE

VIA VOLTERRANA

In midsummer the roadsides are flanked with bright blue irises, the *fluore de-luce* of Florence, as Gerard named it in his *Grete Herball* of 1633. He went on to describe how the dried roots were sold in shops and 'generally everywhere . . . whereof sweet water, sweet powders, and such like are made'. The manufacture of orris root powder was a major rural industry, and it is still widely used in the making of potpourri, the powder acting as a fixative for the perfume of dried flower petals, spices and oils.

In this public rose garden, owned by the city, masses of hybrid teas and floribundas are ranged in carefully tended beds and make a postcard frame for the view of the Duomo and the city of Florence beyond.

SANTO SPIRITO,
FLORENCE

Small private gardens such as
this are hidden behind the
palazzos. The box-edged beds,
fruit trees (in this case ripe
persimmons hang on the
branches of an old tree), and
garlands of variegated ivy and
wistaria, form a tapestry whose
hues and textures recall the silk
brocades and velvets of
Renaissance textiles.

LUNGARNO, FLORENCE

The Lungarni, the streets on
each side of the river Arno
which runs through Florence,
are softened by the *cortile* and
pensile gardens of the hotels,
palazzos and apartments which
line their way. Here, a mop-
headed date palm rears up
above a wistaria trained along
the balustrade-topped wall.

VIA SANT' AGOSTINO,
FLORENCE

A terrace garden is a riot of springtime colour with banks of pot-grown azaleas. These are followed by roses grown as standards and climbers, lavender and iris so that this tiny city garden is rarely without colour. Shaded by a canvas awning, it is the perfect place to sip Pinot Grigio after a hard day's work photographing the gardens of rural Tuscany.

VIA SANT' AGOSTINO,
FLORENCE

A typical Florentine courtyard garden that has recently been renovated by new owners, incorporates the original box-edged beds around the central fountain. The garden is circled by a pergola over which is trained an ancient wistaria. Roses climb the walls and the result is a cool cloister offering welcome refuge from the dusty city streets.

PIAZZA SANTISSIMA ANNUNZIATA
FLORENCE

At the end of April, the piazza in front of the Spedale degli Innocenti is the setting for a flower show, where the growers and nurserymen from the surrounding countryside display and vend their produce. The abundance and variety of the horticultural display is breathtaking seen against the backdrop of the Renaissance orphanage, designed by Brunelleschi and decorated with ten glazed roundels by Andrea della Robbia. It is said that the Florentines regard themselves as the most cultured of the Italians, a notion given credence by the understated opulence of this scene.

Perhaps the most intriguing display of the flower show for cool-climate gardeners is that of the citrus grower. Lemons, oranges, kumquats, and grapefruit trees in every size from stripling whip to fully trained tree are available to the Florentine city gardener. You trundle home with a determination to mimic this rich display of fruit, foliage and fragrance, for nothing outdoes the scent of orange blossom. And the yearning to slip just one small plant in the suitcase to bring back the flavour of a Tuscan garden is unquenchable.

GIARDINO CORSI
FLORENCE

The writer Iris Origo wrote in *The Merchant of Prato*, 1957, that 'Tuscan cities have held their arms wide open to the country' and that in the earliest days it was often difficult to tell 'where the one ended and the other began', as the orchards and gardens flourished right up to and within the city walls. The garden of the Annalena Convent, now known as the Giardino Corsi after the man who built the villa in the 17th century, covers the remains of the earth ramparts built by Cosimo I in 1530, which formed Florence's second line of defence. Surrounded by high walls and linked to the sophisticated Boboli Gardens, it is an unpretentious oasis of tranquillity in which formal elements like this clipped box scroll contrast pleasantly with well-grown stone pines, cypress and ilex.

The tall trees of the Annalena provide a cool shaded spot on this terrace. From here it is possible to view the rest of the gardens, which slope gently down from the highest level behind the house to a distant corner where there are fountains, a *limonaia* and an aviary. The garden was originally the kitchen garden of the Convent of the Annalena, and was designed *c*. 1700 by the architect Manetti. Ferdinand III decreed that excess water from the Boboli fountains could be diverted to water these gardens.

VILLA CORSI
SALVIATI
SESTO FIORENTINO

When the Marchese Giulio Guicciardini Corsi Salviati inherited the villa and garden in 1907, 'the entire site was crowded with a palimpsest of garden styles, ranging from those of the mid-17th century to the late 19th century', wrote Georgina Masson. Now the most obvious relics are, at the western end, the remnants of a *Seicento* water terrace (altered in 1708), and the wilderness at the eastern end of the garden, where in 1868 the *bosco* was given an 'English' treatment. At that time the central parterres were also given the elaborate pattern of diamonds and triangles that we see today.

The Marchese wrote, 'I took warning from the mania that possesses some people for redoing our villas and gardens too much, and in their desire to bring them back to one period, they deprive gardens of the traces left by the passage of time, that gives them a human and living character.' In 1922, with the help of the American architect Harold Donaldson Eberlein, the Marchese undertook the restoration and improvement of the gardens, beginning with the reclamation of the formal *aiuole de bossolo* (box parterre) laid out before the south front of the villa.

Unfortunately, the long canal and semicircular fishponds which form the water terrace are today choked with lilies, and are not the shimmering sheets of water that were originally intended to provide a textural contrast to the adjacent floral parterre.

In 1935, the wilderness, seen here beyond the parterre, was restored to a formal pattern and a pool placed at its centre on an axis with the central pool of the parterre. The pool was surrounded by quartered beds, and a head-high maze of box was planted on the southern side. A grass bowling green was also restored in its original position and a small box-walled theatre planted at the eastern end of the villa adjacent to the wilderness.

93

The interior fountain of the villa *cortile* has been placed on an axis with the theatre and the central fountain of the parterre. This is a typical treatment for a *cortile* and serves as a link between the garden rooms and the dwelling.

SCARPERIA

All traditional Tuscan gardens of whatever size contain an arbour – a shady sitting out area furnished with simple chairs and a table where evening meals can be enjoyed on hot summer evenings. The arbours take many forms; from trees trained and clipped to make leafy enclosures to simple structures like this metal framework, roofed with bamboo matting, over which variegated ivy is trained to merge the arbour with the garden setting.

VILLA GAMBERAIA
SETTIGNANO

The most familiar aspect of the garden is the water parterre, which retains its 15th-century quartered plan, and when viewed from the loggia above can be compared to a Persian carpet. In the early 1900s, Princess Ghika purchased the villa, and with a stroke of genius replaced the flower and vegetable beds of the parterre with pools of water. Is is said that the princess, having lost her beauty to old age, would emerge from the villa only at night to bathe in the still waters of the garden. Since this photograph was taken, the jar-shaped topiary along the left-hand side has been removed and replaced by orange trees in terracotta urns. This has given the parterre a feeling of greater space and emphasised the delicacy of its plan.

Laid out on a terraced hillside site, the garden provides views of the nearby village and beyond, through the summer haze, to the domes and towers of Florence. There are seven distinctly different garden areas: the water parterre, the grotto, the lemon terrace, two *boschi*, a long grass avenue or bowling green and the nymphaeum. The buildings include the villa – a fine example of traditional Tuscan architecture, a chapel, the gatekeeper's lodgings and a *limonaia*, where the many potted citrus trees are overwintered. The villa is approached along an avenue of stately cypress, and, in true Renaissance fashion, the fields and groves of the surrounding *poderi* come right up to the walls of the garden.

Today the box and cypress hedges are studded with standard roses and orange trees. This gives vertical emphasis to the low masses of clipped box which in their maturity contribute a mysterious maze-like quality to the planting. Through their fragrant, dusty branches the cool stillness of the shining pools is glimpsed, the contrast of textures adding to the movement and harmony of the garden scene.

At the far end of the water parterre is a semicircular pool created from the original oval fish pond. The surrounding palisade of clipped cypress is backed by a solid hedge and arbour of climbing roses. It forms a semicircular loggia – as advocated by Alberti to give shelter from cold winds but allowing enjoyment of the sun during winter, and in the summer providing a shady retreat from the sun-drenched parterre.

The long grass avenue with the nymphaeum at its far end separates the villa and parterre from the upper terrace of the garden. It is bordered on one side by the walls of the villa and gatekeeper's house and on the other the retaining walls of the upper terrace. At the opposite end of the avenue is a stone balustrade revealing a distant view of Florence. In spring the pot-grown azaleas ranged against the retaining walls blaze with colour below the cypress and ilex trees of the *bosco*.

The garden clings to its hillside site, the various terraces like the decks of a ship. The long grass avenue ends at a balustrade from which can be enjoyed, as if from the ship's prow, an open view over the countryside and the olive groves of the surrounding *poderi* to the domes and towers of Florence beyond.

Midway down the avenue and directly opposite the back entrance to the villa is the grotto. Stairs on either side of the fountain lead up to the lemon terrace and to a second small *bosco* of ilex trees. The grotto, like the nymphaeum, is typically decorated with pebble mosaic, stucco relief, and rusticated trimmings of tufa and stalactite. These were both expertly restored in the early 1950s by a local craftsman who still practised the traditional skills.

During the Second World War the villa was burned by the retreating German army, and Allied shelling devastated the garden. The late Dr Marchi acquired the property shortly after the end of the war and began restoration. The hedges and topiary which had vanished in the holocaust began to sprout from the blackened stumps, guiding the planting of new material. All care was taken to retain the original 18th-century layout and much attention was given to detail – as in the renovation of the grotto. Today, the gardens of Gamberaia provide the garden visitor with a most sublime pleasure and a profound insight into the history of Tuscan landscape design, and how it has informed the development of the garden styles of England and America.

VILLA CAPPONI
ARCETRI

This charming and exclusively private garden is another example of a perfectly preserved 16th-century Tuscan garden. Built in 1572 by Gino Capponi, the gardens and renovations to the original building were designed to command stunning views of Florence and the valley of the Arno and to provide a healthful, sunny aspect. There are several different garden areas: a lemon terrace and a sunken garden (shown here), which lies below the dainty walled garden and is a 20th-century addition. The garden rooms are united by a grass avenue which extends the length of the villa.

As at Gamberaia, a grass avenue such as this was considered an important, health-inducing part of the garden. Here the family could play bowls and other outdoor games or simply promenade in the fresh air. It also served to link the garden rooms to the house, much as a hallway unites the rooms of a building.

VILLA PALMIERI
FIESOLE

This 15th-century villa is reputed to have inspired Boccaccio's description of the garden in the Third Day of the *Decameron*, where the lords and ladies of the tale sought refuge from the plague. The garden he described was laid out to one side of the palace, traversed by arbours clad in vines, roses and jasmine. In the centre a flowery mead 'spangled with a thousand different flowers and set with cedar and orange trees' surrounded a marble fountain which fed a series of canals and cascades. 'The sight of this garden, its form and contrivance, . . . they spared not to say, if there was a paradise on earth, it could be in no other form.'

This garden room is a perfect example of what a *giardino segreto* should be. It is entirely filled with box-edged beds of single dahlias surrounded by sun-warmed walls festooned with wistaria, jasmine and roses. Originally it could only be reached by a subterranean passage from the house and so was probably intended for use during cold but sunny winter days.

Purchased in 1454 by Marco Palmieri, whose relative Matteo was a leading light in Cosimo I's circle of Platonists, the villa passed into English hands early in the 1760s, when it was bought by the third Earl Cowper, a cultured man who patronized the arts and sciences. The Earl of Crawford and Balcarres purchased the villa in 1874, and in restoring its fabric also set about enlarging and 'improving' the garden so that it 'combined the beauty of an Italian garden with the care and order of an English home'. From this well-ordered terrace there is a fine view over the garden below and across the broad lawns planted with specimen trees.

The oldest part of the garden to survive Lord Crawford's improvements is this charming oval lemon garden, laid out in 1697 by Palmerio Palmieri, and clearly shown in an 18th-century engraving by Zocchi. Norah Lindsay, the English garden designer and friend of Lawrence Johnston of Hidcote Manor, was married to the Earl's nephew. She claimed an intimate knowledge of Italian gardens, and may well have cultivated her love affair from the historic gardens of Villa Palmieri. The design of her own garden at Sutton Courtenay Manor near Oxford showed a marked Italianate influence, as did the many other gardens on which she advised, including Vita Sackville-West's first garden at Long Barn.

The broad lawns of the Victorian gardens are seen here from the terrace, overlooking the Baroque lemon garden. Queen Victoria was twice the Earl's guest, once in 1888 when she planted a cypress, and again in 1893.

RIPOSO DEI VESCOVI
FIESOLE

The once grand gardens of this private villa were created during the late 1920s by a Dutch artist, Nieuwenkamp, who had joined the ranks of the expatriate population in the hills of Fiesole to pursue his dream of Italy. Following the prevailing trend for newcomers to recreate and restore gardens according to the traditional Tuscan pattern, he created a series of garden rooms opening off the main axis of a cypress avenue and overlooked by a wistaria-clad loggia. Both purple and white varieties grow here, making a splendid springtime display.

Pergolas shaded by Banksian roses, box topiary and hedges decorate the garden rooms, whose lawns are now carpets of wild flowers and rough grass. So many of the gardens from this period are showing their age, due to the expense of their upkeep, the amount of labour involved in sustaining yard upon yard of clipped box and the vagaries of the Tuscan climate. But even in their decay there is still the spark of romance and the image of faded grandeur that have caused many cold northern hearts to flutter.

The villa is built on the site of the old staging post where bishops travelling from Florence to their summer villas at Fiesole would stop to rest and change carriages. The villa, like the garden, is built on several levels, following the contour of the hillside, and commands extensive views of the garden, which is laid out in a series of terraces connected by this central avenue. The fountain halfway down its length is decorated with oriental forms reflecting Nieuwenkamp's close ties with the Dutch East Indies.

VIA VOLTERRANA

In an *orti di famigilia*, or kitchen garden, just outside the city on the old Volterra road, onions, garlic and broad-leaved parsley grow, recalling Iris Origo's description in her book *The Merchant of Prato* of Margherita's kitchen garden in 1410: 'Onions, too, and garlic gave savour to almost every dish – the latter forming the basis of a sauce called agliata – and Margherita's garden, like that of every other careful housewife, was also rich in mint, stonewort, thyme, marjoram and rosemary.' Family gardens have not changed that much in five hundred years; small beds are devoted to a single vegetable or herb, fruit and olive trees shade the borders, and roses are always present.

VIA VECCHIA FIESOLANA

Alerted to the existence of this *orto di familigia* by the wildly exotic *Albizia julibrissin* flaunting its flowers over the top of the garden wall, we were welcomed into the small enclosed garden. Every inch of space was utilized for flowers and vegetables, grown in small beds surrounded by a path lined with herbs and ornamental shrubs. Around the foundations of the old house, the Tuscan equivalent of an Elizabethan country cottage, were pots of basil, box cuttings and vegetable seedlings.

VILLA SCHIFANOIA
FIESOLE

In 1927 this estate, which dates from the 16th century, became the property of a wealthy American expatriate, Myron C. Taylor, who served as US ambassador to the Vatican during the time of Pope Pius XII. Taylor completely restored the villa to house his art collection and created the extensive formal gardens on the gentle slopes around the villa. The garden is terraced into three elegant grass-filled box parterres ranged around a series of small pools and fountains.

The small lily pool on the uppermost terrace marks the divergence of the main axis. From here you either descend to the parterre shown opposite or to a less elaborate one on a lower level, in which a fountain recessed into a stairwell once provided music.

GIARDINO DELLA GHERARDESCA
FLORENCE

This secret and very private garden in the heart of Florence began as a formal Renaissance villa garden, dating from 1472, but in 1800 was made over into a romantic English-style landscape park. Many specimen trees were planted then which have now reached their maturity, including a rare and wonderful coloured sumac and a fine *Ginkgo biloba*, not to mention many excellent *Magnolia grandiflora*.

Many other trees, mostly limes and ilex, shade the park. This charming temple, designed by Giuseppe Cacialli, was added in 1842. The gardens have recently undergone restoration, following a programme devised by Pietro Porcinai in which he referred more obviously to the *genii loci* of the site than the English landscaping had done. The result is a park which is more at ease in its urban setting, but which because of its exclusive privacy retains the mystery and romanticism of earlier days.

SAN DOMENICO, FIESOLE

An ancient olive tree, its trunk
split open, perhaps by frost or
else simply by age, sprouts
anew from its base. The
gardens of Tuscany are as
much about small details as
grand compositions. Thoughts
are focused by vignettes such as
this, where the rejuvenation of
the olive parallels the tenacious
existence of the old Tuscan
gardens, which have survived
through centuries of
momentous change, not
because of pressure from
preservation societies but
because of the conservative
nature of the Tuscan people.

GIARDINO CAPPONI
FLORENCE

This is a classic example of a
lemon garden laid out in
elegant formality before a
charming Baroque *limonaia*,
where during the winter the
citrus trees are stored in their
huge terracotta pots to protect
them from the hard frosts.
Stone plinths dotted along the
paths await the return of the
potted trees.

SETTIGNANO

Just under five miles east of the city centre of Florence, the sunflower fields of Settignano flourish amid groves of olives and vineyards. The charm of Settignano's rural setting and the views of Florence from the hill on which it rests have beckoned generations of artists and writers. The Villa Buonarroti is said to have been Michelangelo's childhood home, Mark Twain wrote *Pudd'nhead Wilson* while living in the village and the art historian Bernard Berenson and his wife Mary pursued their dream of the aesthetic life from their villa, I Tatti.

I TATTI
SETTIGNANO

Bernard and Mary Berenson were renting I Tatti in 1906, when Geoffrey Scott and Maynard Keynes were introduced to their circle as companions for Mary's two young daughters. A year later the architect Cecil Pinsent met the Berensons while he was on tour in Italy, during which time he began work on the Villa Gattaia in Florence for Charles Loeser. Mary remarked that he seemed 'nice, but not very exciting'. However, he made sufficient impression for the Berensons to commission him in 1909 to transform their house and garden, after an Italian architect had let them down. They also persuaded Geoffrey Scott to join him in the work. Mary wrote, 'Cecil's ideas . . . were excellent, but his control of the Italian workmen left much to be desired; Geoffrey had excellent taste, but his health and energy were minimal.'

The 'Artichokes', as the Berensons called their young architects, lived and worked at the villa almost continuously for the next two years. The main gardens were laid out on a south-facing slope in a series of gentle terraces reached through the *limonaia*. The terrace between the house and the *limonaia* is planted with box-edged beds, which in summer contain pure white impatiens. The trees in the centre of the beds add vertical interest at all times of the year. It was Pinsent's habit to make Plasticine models of his projects, which reinforced the strong architectural origins of his garden schemes. I Tatti was designed as a series of outdoor rooms to provide Bernard Berenson, 'BB' as he was known, with a wide variety of landscapes in which to walk – his favourite pastime.

There were times when Mary despaired of her championing of Pinsent, who was 'wildly spendthrift and entirely unregulated, . . . you cannot make him run on the rails of commonsense'. Pinsent perceived himself as '. . . practical, inventive with an aptitude for things visible to the eye, but dumb [inarticulate]'. He was certainly fluent with the principles of the Renaissance garden and based the parterres on 15th- and 16th-century designs. The terraces are enclosed on both sides by walls of tall clipped cypress and parallel walks shaded by avenues of ilex. Behind the villa a *pensile* garden forms a secret corner of more clipped-box patterning, and there is another walk shaded by evergreen trees and fenced with trailing wistaria.

Sir Kenneth Clark wrote in his memoirs that it was under the influence of Cecil Pinsent that Mary Berenson had 'constructed an imitation Baroque garden', which Bernard had always disliked, 'but it was below the rustic *limonaia* that he sat and talked after luncheon'. Descending to the terraces from the house front, the main axis of the garden runs through the centre of the lemon house, its arched entrance framing a view of the garden.

Walking the hillsides of Fiesole and Settignano was Berenson's relaxation and he was familiar with every path. Each walk was given a name; some for friends who had discovered them. Pinsent successfully merged the formal garden with the surrounding landscape by creating a series of tree-lined avenues leading into the rugged countryside. Such shaded avenues surrounding the formal gardens serve the same purpose as the vine-laden arbours and pergolas which framed the Medici gardens of the Renaissance.

Berenson once expressed a wish that he could return to haunt I Tatti, so much did he love the house that so precisely expressed his 'needs, tastes and aspirations'. However, his portrait bust brings him back to the garden, which, despite opinions to the contrary, he also cherished. He wrote, 'I have a garden too . . . Unless it pours with rain, I run through it at least once a day, to taste the air, to listen to the sound of birds and streams, to admire the flowers and trees.'

LE BALZE
FIESOLE

As Cecil Pinsent's work on I Tatti was nearing completion, he was commissioned by Charles Augustus Strong, another American expatriate and a friend of the Berensons, to design his new villa and garden at Fiesole. Work began on the villa in 1912 and on the garden in 1913, continuing for six years. Le Balze was Pinsent's first major architectural commission, but his third garden, and is the one in which his profound understanding of the placing of buildings within the landscape is most ably displayed. The property is located on a hillside, the garden plan being longitudinal, with the villa sited approximately at the centre of two horizontal parallel axes from which the sequence of garden rooms is entered. The eastern end of the villa overlooks the winter garden, photographed from the loggia of the guest apartments.

The wall below the loggia overlooking the winter garden is covered in the climber *Trachelospermum jasminoides*, the star jasmine. The perfume from this evergreen climber, combined with the scent of lemon flowers from the parterre, fills the walled enclosure and wafts through the open windows into the room behind the loggia.

From the street entrance, at the eastern end of the property, the first garden room encountered is the orange garden, but the trees were lost to freezing weather and Strong replaced them with trailing pelargoniums trained over wire frames. From here the main axis of the garden continues westward through the winter garden, across the villa entrance and past the fountain grotto, eventually emerging at the *bosco*. Above this path is an elevated pergola-covered walk, draped in *Rosa banksiae* 'Lutea'. The secondary axis runs below the villa, linking the formal garden areas at the eastern end with the 'wild garden' on the western side, and was originally a sequence of open and enclosed spaces.

Pinsent was reponsible for designing and making much of the *rocaille* decorations in the gardens he landscaped. Le Balze is particularly well endowed with these: Pinsent wrote that in 1921 he made two river gods, two Hermes and four portrait busts of Greek philosophers to decorate the garden. The fountain grotto, which was made on the site of the original entrance to the property, is entirely Pinsent's work and is the third formal area encountered along the main axis after the orange garden and winter garden. Stairs on either side of the fountain lead to the elevated pergola walk. Other decoration in the garden, such as stone mosaics, tufa work, stalactites and stucco relief, is mostly Pinsent's work. The medallion to the fountain's right is Pinsent's self-portrait.

The main axis ends in the tiny grove of ilex which forms the shady *bosco* on the other side of the villa, the path leading to another of Pinsent's rusticated grottoes. The trees of the *bosco* are set in a quincunx, which perfectly echoes the formality of the garden rooms at the opposite end of the path, but without the ornate pattern of a parterre and floral planting. This scheme ensures that the garden devolves gently from the organized architectural space of the street entrance into the natural landscape of meadow and olive grove at its furthermost boundaries.

Today, the secondary axis ends
in a vista of cypress, olives and
recently planted plane trees, its
gravel path bordered by
contemporary plantings of
Florentine iris and lavender.
The hillside below the villa and
adjacent to the olive grove is
planted with spring-flowering
plums and lilacs, and
ornamentals such as *Paulownia
fargesii*, *Acer platanoides*
'Crimson King' and bushes of
Cotinus coggygria to provide a
year-round display. The
gardens were damaged during
the Second World War, but its
restoration was supervised by
Pinsent, who, with the rank of
Captain, was serving with the
Monuments and Fine Arts
section of the Allied Military
Government in Italy. In 1979,
Le Balze was donated to
Georgetown University by
Margaret Strong de Larrain,
Dr Strong's daughter. It is
strictly private and not open to
the general public.

LA PIETRA
FLORENCE

The villa of La Pietra dates in
part from the *Quattrocento*, but
the gardens are of this century,
the result of a 'Tuscanizing'
that began in 1904, when
Arthur Acton, father of the
present owner, Sir Harold
Acton, acquired the property
and set about recreating the
original gardens 'as he imagined
they might have been', as a
setting for his collection of
classical sculpture. The central
axis runs eastwards from the
garden front of the villa across
the central parterre with its
graceful pool and fountain to
the lower parterre.

The staircase leads to the lower parterre – an open sunny amphitheatre of clipped-box hedges and statuary, bordered on the western side by a stone pergola hung with purple-flowered wistaria. The garden extends north and south of the central axis in a series of garden rooms, each with its own character of light and shade, warm sun and cool shadow, but always enriched with fine ornament.

In his book *The Villas of Tuscany* Sir Harold wrote that 'in no other private Florentine garden have I seen statues of such individual strength and grace, from the lone colossus by Orazio Marinali to the Venetian figures by Francesco Bonazza which have stepped onto the open air theatre as for one of Goldoni's comedies'. The paths leading to the theatre or the colossus are marked at their crossing by other fine statues, and the eye is rewarded for following a vista by careful architectural and sculptural compositions such as this.

There is little floral decoration at La Pietra to compete with the splendour of the sculpture collection. Creamy Banksian roses, mauve wistaria, pink pelargoniums and climbing roses trained against retaining walls are permitted, but the sombre yews and fragrant box in their clipped architectural forms are the chief support of the garden scheme.

Box and cypress perfume the air, convent bells, birdsong and the croak of frogs in the lily pool fill the garden rooms with quiet music; soft turf and hard gravel, warm stone and cool moss, shade and sun mark the progression from one heart-rending vista to another. This is a thoroughly sensual garden, paced to the contemplation of beauty.

The *giardino segreto* to the north of the villa is a walled lemon garden, its formal beds studded with terracotta urns holding citrus trees; the beds themselves are planted with vegetables.

VIA DELLA FONTE, FLORENCE

In a cloistered garden, calendula, antirrhinums, stocks and countless other simple flowers have seeded in the paths and flowerbeds beneath goblet-trained fruit trees and espaliered vines, transforming an otherwise small dull courtyard into the *hortus conclusus* (enclosed garden) of the *Trecento*.

PALAZZO CORSINI
SUL PRATO
FLORENCE

The formal gardens of this
Florentine palace are well
hidden by their high walls.
Low box hedges make intricate
patterns, the interstices filled
with grey santolina that echoes
the colour of the stone
sculptures lining the main axis
of the garden.

VIA GUICCIARDINI,
FLORENCE

A collection of archaeological
artefacts has been used to good
effect to decorate the walls of a
small city garden.

GIARDINO TORRIGIANI
FLORENCE

The grounds of this exclusively private garden, along with the much smaller Annalena and the vast gardens of the Boboli, form a cluster around the Porta Romana. These gardens provide a green pocket in the centre of the Oltrarno district where the artisans and tradesmen who supply the exclusive shops of Florence live and work.

Today the Principessa Torrigiani describes how her ancestor purchased an entire quarter of the Oltrarno district of Florence, moved the people out and levelled their homes to make way for his fashionable garden. The famous tower was built on a mound made from the rubble; the structure itself has an iconography relating to the history of the family and each level corresponds to the height of a significant building, such as the summit of the Duomo.

VILLA GINORI
SESTO FIORENTINO

The grounds around the villa, which dates from 1525, include a botanical garden and glasshouse which was used to grow pineapples and other rare and exotic plants, and a large landscaped park laid out in the 19th century by Marchese Carlo Leopoldo Ginori. He was responsible for founding the factory in a nearby villa which evolved into the world-famous Ginori china industry.

The oldest part of the garden dates from between 1616 and 1620, when the gardens nearest the old villa were laid out by Lionardo Ginori in a series of formal beds of *semplici*, stocked with the flowers and herbs used for herbal remedies. These gardens today retain much of their original character and are decorated with the familiar orange and lemon trees in terracotta urns typical of traditional Tuscan gardens.

VILLA VILLORESI
SESTO FIORENTINO

'One side of my house was a
much neglected but lovely little
square, walled garden. . . . The
beds and paths . . . were of a
simple formal pattern, which
gave great dignity to the weedy
little wilderness; and there
were the usual terracotta pots
with strong, well-grown
Lemon-trees in them, the pride
of the Tuscan peasant's heart.
The flowers on them scented
the air; the peasants sell the
pale fruit at a special price all
the summer through in the
town as we sell glass-grown
peaches. I think that if we tried
to grow plants of this sort of
Lemon at home in pots or tubs,
it would be far better than
trying to grow the more delicate
Oranges usually seen on
terraces in England', wrote Mrs
Earle in *More Pot Pourri from a
Surrey Garden*, 1899, and a
scene such as this could have
been her inspiration.

IL ROSETO
FLORENCE

This garden, designed in 1965
by the great modern landscape
designer, Pietro Porcinai, is his
most famous domestic work.
His philosophy was strongly
influenced by the humanist
thinking of the Renaissance,
and he strove in his gardens to
create harmony between man
and his environment by
constructing landscapes that
evoke the atmosphere of
tranquillity found in the old
Tuscan gardens of the
Quattrocento and *Cinquecento*.
From the villa and the elevated
formal parterre garden spread
before it there is a panoramic
view; to one side it is of the
distant city while in the other
direction the natural landscape
of the Val d'Ema is framed by
the informal rose garden set in a
grove of olives. Thus the
garden elements relate directly
to the view they are framing.

The formal parterre is translated into modern shapes, the geometry of the 16th century giving way to curvilinear box hedges, alternating with circles of grass and wells, through one of which grows a mature ilex tree. Plane trees planted above supporting columns frame the distant view of the city. The thought and engineering involved in the creation of this *pensile* garden were truly Renaissance in their scope.

The garden is entered from the street through a vine-covered pergola leading into a parking area which is below the parterre garden. The massed concrete shell of this spacious area is domed, and decorated with circular pebble-mosaic patterns that echo the patterns of box and grass overhead. The spiral stone staircase leading to the villa and garden is suspended by steel rods and curtained with ivy; at its base a fountain splashes into a circular pool.

FRATELLI MASINI
IMPRUNETA

Terracotta urns, tubs and pots planted with orange and lemon trees have been a characteristic feature of Tuscan gardens since medieval times, and Impruneta, an ancient Etruscan settlement, has traditionally been the centre of their production. *Quadro* or square work (bricks and tiles) and *tondo* or round work (urns etc.) were produced during this century by more than twenty firms. Today only six remain and Masini Brothers are the last to produce only *tondo*. The pots are hand-formed either from paste spread over a mould, or from mould-cast sections, or free-form by smoothing lumps of clay in layers over a mould. The raw clay is dug from the surrounding hillsides in boulders which are pulverized and the dust or *terra* mixed with water to make the malleable clay.

The *tondo* are fired for two days in vast wood-fuelled kilns at a temperature of 960–70°C, which entails a constant vigil. They are then cooled, evenly to prevent cracking, for four days to a week. It is laborious, poorly paid work and at one time, as with many old skills, there was a fear that it would die out as the older artisans retired. But now an apprentice school has opened and that day has been forestalled. What would a Tuscan garden be without its lovely terracotta furnishings?

PHOTOGRAPHER'S NOTES

When embarking on any photographic project, before even thinking of what equipment and techniques might be appropriate, one needs a thorough familiarity with the subject to be illustrated. For that, it helps to be able to work in harmony with a well-informed author, and in the present case there was nothing easier.

The Tuscan landscape we set out to describe and illustrate is one greatly indebted to the people who have lived there; for centuries they have been shaping its contours, impressing a variety of geometrical patterns onto the highly diversified terrain that ranges from the Apennine mountains and the Apuan Alps (pockmarked white by their famous marble quarries) through, lower down, the Sienese hills, where vineyards and olive groves seem almost traced out by a master draughtsman's hand, to, lower still, the gentle verdant valleys of the Lucca region. The land everywhere is fragmented into a myriad properties large and small, many of which have taken shape in the distant past and most of which have an area set aside for a garden or park, whether large or small, monumental or intimate.

When it comes to photographing gardens, if you really wish to conjure up some of their poetic reality, you should ideally be able to linger there for hours, on the alert for the perfect moment when the sun is low on the horizon and the sky just flecked with clouds, when the light is exactly right and not too harsh, yet strong enough to model the architecture of tree and plant, which vary so much from one garden to another.

Alas, this is not always possible. Permission to photograph is granted days in advance, if not weeks, and for a brief time only, sometimes for no more than an hour. It is useless to appeal to the goddess Fortuna for help: she is blind and, when a herd of photographers clamour all at once for her attention, each with a different idea for the view to be taken, deaf.

Because of such limitations on time, along with the difficulties of getting from one place to another whilst the sun is still right – lovely car rides often, but not always easy – it seemed best to rely on photographic equipment in small format, not burdensome to carry and quick to set up and put into operation.

The best camera for this purpose proved to be the Leica M5 with 21 mm, 35 mm, and 50 mm lenses. The Leica is not subject to the same vibration as the single-lens reflex camera, since it has no mirror mechanism and the lens diaphragm is already set. This meant that I could work with slow shutter speeds down to 1/15th of a second without having to employ a tripod. In certain cases I shifted to a Pentax XL so as to be able to profit from an old 40 mm Pentax lens, which is closest to the perspective of the human eye, and also so as to use long-focus lenses which are not convenient with a Leica M5.

Most of the time I used 25 ISO and 64 ISO Kodachrome professional film, but in autumn, because of the low light conditions, I resorted to Ektachrome 100 ISO professional film pushed to 200 ISO, which allowed me to close down a stop, thus ensuring greater depth of field as well as slightly warmer tones in the colour development. On some occasions it was necessary to utilise a small Gitzo tripod.

With the atmosphere of the gardens my chief concern, I did not worry overmuch about distortions resulting from the use of wide-angle lenses. Occasionally, where I considered it really necessary to minimise distortions, I adopted the Silvestre 6 × 7 lens shift camera with a 47 mm Schneider lens, which also allowed me greater control over the final composition of the photograph.

GARDENS OPEN TO THE PUBLIC

While many of the gardens featured on these pages are strictly private – and the authors would ask that this be respected – the major gardens, listed below, are open to the public, generally from 9 to 12 a.m. and again from 2 to 5 p.m. and for varying entrance fees. Gardens owned by the *comune* – shown here with a (c) – are usually closed for one day a week, often Mondays. Check with the local tourist agency for details.

Siena area
Orti Leonini, San Quivico d'Orcia (c)
Palazzo Piccolomini, Pienza

Lucca area
Villa Garzoni, Collodi (c)
Villa Mansi, Segromigno
Villa Torrigiani, Camigliano

Florence area
Giardino di Boboli, Florence (c)
Parco Demidoff, Pratolino (c)
Villa Gamberaia, Settignano
Villa Medici, Castello (c)
Villa Medici, Fiesole
Villa Petraia, Castello (c)
La Pietra, Florence
Giardino delle Rose, Florence (c)

Agriturist – Piazza S. Firenze 3, Florence (tel: 28 18 38) – operates an excellent programme of bus tours of the major gardens around Florence and Lucca throughout the week from April to June. The leaflet providing details of these tours is available from the office given above or from tourist agencies in Florence and from most hotel concierges.

BIBLIOGRAPHY

Acton, Sir Harold *The Villas of Tuscany*, Thames and Hudson, revised ed. 1987

Berenson, Bernard *Sketch for a Self-Portrait*, Constable, 1949; *Sunset and Twilight*, Hamish Hamilton, 1964

Clark, Sir Kenneth *Another Part of the Wood*, John Murray, 1974

Frith, Ian J.W. 'Porcinai; Renaissance in the Italian Garden', *Landscape Architecture*, vol. 72 no. 2, 1984

Jellicoe, Sir Geoffrey 'Italian Renaissance Gardens' *Journal of the Royal Society of Arts*, 6 Feb., 1953; *Italian Gardens of the Renaissance*, Ernest Benn, 1925

McCarthy, Mary *The Stones of Florence*, Heinemann, 1959

Masson, Georgina *Italian Gardens*, Thames and Hudson 1961; *Italian Villas and Palaces*, Thames and Hudson, 1959; 'Florentine and Tuscan Gardens', *Apollo*, vol. 100 no. 151, 1974

Origo, Iris *Merchant of Prato*, Jonathan Cape, 1957; *Images and Shadows*, Century, 1984

Strachey, Barbara and Samuels, Jayne ed. *Mary Berenson; a Self-Portrait*, Victor Gollancz, 1983

Walker D.S. *A Geography of Italy*, Methuen, 2nd ed., 1967

Wharton, Edith *Italian Villas and Their Gardens*, Century, New York, 1904

INDEX